Her, Infinite

New Issues Poetry & Prose

Editor	William Olsen
Guest Editor	Nancy Eimers
Managing Editor	Kimberly Kolbe
Layout Editor	Sarah Kidd
Assistant Editor	Iliana Rocha

New Issues Poetry & Prose
The College of Arts and Sciences
Western Michigan University
Kalamazoo, MI 49008

First Edition, 2016.
Second printing, 2017.

ISBN-13   978-1-936970-41-4 (paperbound)

Library of Congress Cataloging-in-Publication Data:
Morris, Sawnie.
Her, Infinite/Sawnie Morris
Library of Congress Control Number   2015915437

Art Director	Nicholas Kuder
Designer	Emilee Guzak
Production Manager	Paul Sizer
	The Design Center, Frostic School of Art
	College of Fine Arts
	Western Michigan University
Printing	Maple Press

Her, Infinite

Sawnie Morris

New Issues Press

WESTERN MICHIGAN UNIVERSITY

for my beloved, Brian

Contents

I.

II.

III.

IV.

Acknowledgments

Grateful acknowledgment is made to the following publications in which poems from *Her, Infinite* first appeared:

Chokecherries, Denver Quarterly, Journal of Feminist Studies in Religion, Lana Turner, Malpais Review, Mudfish Review, Pool: A Journal of Poetry, Taos Journal of International Poetry & Art, The Journal, www. drunkenboat.com, Written Here: The Community of Writers Poetry Review 2013

"Cochiti Lake, 1989" was selected by Hettie Jones for the Poetry Society of America George Bogin Memorial Award and subsequently appeared in the *Poetry Society of America 100th Anniversary* program.

"Most Mornings," "How Strange to Wake," "After Having Thought About It for a Long Time," "Little Shifts, Here and There, a Fashion of Change," and "Fallen Moon in the House of Speech" appeared in *The Sound a Raven Makes*, (Tres Chicas Books, 2006).

"I Have Known Her Since My Beginnings in Her Thoughts" is for Sarah Sawnie Robertson.

My most profound and loving gratitude goes to *mi hombre guapo*, Brian Shields, who believed in these poems, who held our world together across my "couch years" (when most of these poems were written), whose art and dedication to his art inspires me at every turn, and whose leadership and courage changed the outcome for the waters of New Mexico. I'd like to thank Nancy Eimers, Bill Olsen, and the entire editorial and design team at New Issues Press. I bow to Major Jackson in gratitude. My heartfelt thanks goes to Christine Hemp, Linda Aldrich, Joan Houlihan, Jeffery Levine, Dawn McGuire, Valerie Martínez, and Lise Goett, each of whose comments helped to shape these poems/this manuscript; to Nancy Laupheimer, Lee Lee, Joan Logghe, Nancy Ryan, and SOMOS for honoring these poems along the way; to Connie Busch, Michael Diaz, Alyce Frank, M.C. Gee, Joan Harvey, E.J. Levy, Tania Oppenheim, and Pat and Larry Sargent for steadying the boat; to Cathy Deely, Gwen Raftery, Mary Humphrey, Nikki Keyser, Jeannine Mestre, Peggy Nelson, John Nichols, Connie Odé, Martha Quintana, John Rutherford, Magdalene Smith, Cathy Strisik, Joni Tickle, and Summer Wood for their unfailing encouragement; to Cathy Cockrell, Linda Fair, Reneé Gregorio, Judy Meyers, Gaia Mika, Pam Shepherd, Lillian Silva, Jeannie Winer, and everybody else who kept showing up (you know who you are); to Ana X Gutierrez Sisneros and Irwin Rivera for the courage of their testimonies; to Andrea Watson and Veronica Golos of 3: A Taos Press for almost taking the manuscript; and to each of the poets and dreamers who participated in my workshops during the time in which these poems were written and thus inspired me. I am grateful to Natalie Goldberg for "writing practice" and to Ralph Angel for "essential language"; to the Colrain Conference and to the Squaw Valley Community of Writers, including Claudia Rankine, whose craft talk inspired the seed poem for this collection, as well as to Forrest Gander and Evie Shockley—and most especially Robert Hass, Sharon Olds, Brenda Hillman, and Galway Kinnel, each of whose abiding presence, even at a distance, sustained me from the start. My thanks go also to Pablo, Anna, Jackson, Wallace, and Nakoi (dog and cat witnesses), and to the apple, pine, cottonwood, and apricot trees for the beauty of their dreaming. I am grateful beyond measure for the blessing of my mother, Sarah Sawnie Smith Robertson, a poet, and my father, Edmund Taylor Morris, Jr., a storyteller, and I extend a gratitude as big as the loving embrace of all of the universes to my younger sisters, Charlton Smith Morris Traynor and Belle Scott Morris Koschnitzke.

Last, I wish to thank Amigos Bravos and Communities for Clean Water for their tenacity and courage, and especially Joni Arends, who whispered, "You need to see this."

even
the beer
and wine bottle shards
the butts and shot gun shells—
that under the usual spell
agitate

find their rightful insignificance
slight signature
of clawed feet
in the corner of
her, infinite

I.

Da-ma-te, Demeter

re: *citizen monitoring of stormwater discharges from Los Alamos National Laboratory, Hillside 140, 2007*

The field before us is open, lit.
Is matted with grass stalk and rivulet.
Is a former landfill. (Filled with what?)
God of the underworld, someone says.
Most of it removed to a locked-down site—but, inevitably—
You'll receive some exposure, someone else says.

She gives me a black box, a *Rad Alert.*
Background radiation at counts per minute is 30.
At 70, it's okay. At 90 or 100, MOVE.

The field before us is open, lit.
Is matted with grass stalk, is sun-striped and crisscrossed with rivulets.

Let us go then, you & I.

Stepping forward stepping forward 70 70 70 (*little stream. meadow ventricle. glittering margin. indentation. lipped & riffed by—*) stepping left 85 86 stepping forward 79 75 (*stiff gold stems. excavation. sprawl of hairgrass. manna grass. blue grass. rabbit-foot grass. barley. giant reed.*) stepping right 75 79 85 stepping forward 85 89 90 standing still **95** (*nuclei. nuclei. private half-lives. nuclei. violent decay.*) 89 stepping left 85   stepping forward **89**   **90** stepping right 85 stepping right 75 standing still (*digital snap of cameras. sediment samplers. the pine. its dark viridian. don't be—*) **90** stepping back **97** stepping back **100** stepping back **103** stepping right stepping right **107** (*exclamation point. exclamation point. exclamation point.*) leaping forward leaping left **101 101** leaping left **99** backing up **90** turning around hurrying back 83 stepping forward (*splay of sod-song. dank dishevelment. dormant. seed.*) 76 75 76 standing still an island 72 70 standing still breathing in breathing out breathing in breathing out

13

You know what worries me? our guide asks. It's flying in planes.
That's what worries me. She looks away, angles her chin
down, shakes
her hair. The field

is such a lovely
field.

The field
is such an open

field.

The field is full of light. Full of life.

This field is home to canyon frog and rattle snake… .To cowbird and
mourning dove .. This field is home to bushtit and bluebird …To
grossbill.. American crow..and gopher.. . To deer mouse and warbler
and black bear and bob cat. .. This field is crossed by chipmunk and
mule deer..by coyote and grey fox and red fox and lion and raccoon..
..It's home to porcupine..to bushy-tailed rat and white-throated rat..and
ringtail and shrew ..to spruce snail and glass snail..to striped skunk and
pinion jay..mocking bird and elk. .. . This field is food for gold finch
and   goshawk.. grosbeak.. ferruginous hawk ..purple martin.. and
nighthawk.. .This field is food to spotted owl.. ermine weasel.. .golden
mantled squirrel.. ..great horned owl.. dark-eyed junco and saw-whet.. .
It's life to raven and roadrunner and robin and ash-throated fly
catcher.. .sapsucker starling and swallow. ..This field belongs. ..to.
..tanager.. .titmouse.. ..hermit thrush..towhee..wild turkey.. ..wax wing..
 woodpecker .. and vulture. ..And at dusk. .this field is often crossed by
spotted bat and badger .. . ..

Inland See (I)

re: *"Deepwater Horizon" catastrophic oil spill, June, 2010*

i

Who knew the neighbor's bronze egret, silly simulacra
poised above real bugs,
would become so difficult to look at?

ii

We try not to think too much of sea birds
or the car burning its crude, the coastline where we dove into waves,
the salt slung heat and damp littoral sand, pocked armature of sand-dollars
and shiny blue marble of by-the-wind sailors. (Untouchable, translucence.)
Admired how they bloomed where they began, beach-sprung
(so we thought) and moved mysteriously
the way we did. The sandbar distance enough, the Gulf undertow gentle.
Beyond lay an unsullied depth, its blind feeling night creatures
their bioluminescence and phosphorous, penetralia
where *plume* and *embedded* still
belonged to us.

iii

Wave-lace replicates feather-tips and something sudden stirs.
      An awkward dead branch
branches out, impales what glides past. We could almost wish to be torn
in an unhelpful gesture of atonement,
feeling we are
the predicament.

iv

Tattered—our neighbor's flag—red, white, and blue
waves   whip,   rip,   and unravel
in easterly Gulf winds, while everyone
and no one   watches.

Inside a Dream, Inside a Storm to Come

.

some facts of observation. some circumstances of occurrence.
some markings. some peculiar crystallized shape. some nuclear
ice on water. some frost on surface ice. some haze on crops.
some tabular frost. some plume & seaweed frost. some dendrite ice.
some needle ice. some cupflowers in ice. some glaze on vegetation.
some raindrops on the grass. some dew on blade on bee on grass. some
web. some strand. some wetnesses on glassy sleet-rime—STOP

language is the net & it's our job to make it mean, i say
some are more at ease with diving, i say back to me

"the undersurface down in the body of water"
"the slow internal melting under the influence of"
"we occluded as the ice grew thicker"
"we were delicate plumes & patterns of frost"
"we gathered along our abrasions"
"unbroken, infinitesimal surfaces"
"on the walls of our rooms"
"inequalities in the availability of moisture"
"crystals in a herringbone pattern"
"or, at the 90 degree angle of departure"
"of the fir"
"rime is the tufty deposit of ice caused by"
"sudden freeze"
"at the time and place of impact"
"it builds out in the face of the wind"
"—sometimes over-accumulating—"
"even to the crushing of shrubbery & breaking of trees"

Cochiti Lake, 1989

Plank-patterned. Nail-headed.
The waves were silvery. There was a wind.
It was my idea to go there.

It was my idea.

We were liquid. Which is to say,
we were not quite gelled.

It was at Cochiti. Where the Rio Grande pools for a while (before)
        spilling recklessly
                over the dam.

Night came. We lay down in our separate sleeping bags.
Why is this important to you?
We lay down.
We saw a star falling.
In slow motion,
in an arch, a small white dot descending.
Visible only in the moment it fell.

(A flare.)

You told me your wish.

(A risk.)

I remember the fishermen checking their traps. Oaring out to the
center of the lake, entering the realm of its iris. Their silhouettes.
The metal clanging. The dock roughing us up. The dock knocked
about by the waves, the waves by the wind. The smear of thin-ish
clouds filtering moon. The feel of your hand resting (lightly) on the
small of my back.

In the morning, I stripped down to swim. (Water is my medium.)
I did flip turns (w/out a wall) and back bends. I invited you in.
That's when it began. When I invited you

We didn't know the word "aquifer."
We didn't know the phrase "perched water zone."
We didn't know the meaning of "ephemeral stream,"
              its relation to precipitation
                     or the melting of snow.

We didn't know about "impairment," (the available options). The list:
         where we could no longer swim,
         where and what we could no longer drink.
We didn't know about "fluctuating temperature" or "vectors for pathogens."
We didn't know about "turbidity," about "incident light"
and what it might mean to be
         "scattered or absorbed" in sediments. What it might mean

              to become
                     a "*suspended solid*," to be "*alluvial* "
                            to be "eroded, transported, and deposited"
                     by a stream
                            onto a solid rock shelf.

I thought "primary contact" was what happened
                                    between *us*
                                            that night.
(the feel of your hands) (the small of my back)

We didn't know about tritium, strontium -90, or plutonium -238.
We didn't know about unlined pits, trenches, and shafts.

The map of the Pajarito Plateau, with its canyons and springs and flats—
had I seen it—I would have told you it looked like a lung,
at home in the cage of its ribs.

We didn't know about the lit lives of explosives, RDX & HMX.

We didn't know about VOLITAL and SEMI-volatile compounds.
(well, maybe we knew
        a little something of that . . .)

—as we knew a little something
                                    of concentrated metals:

Copper: shiny pan. shade of your skin.
Zinc: raspberry flavored tablet I suck to stop a sore throat.
Lead: dark vein of a pencil. (the tip of it jutting out of my bag
& into my thigh
        when the bus lurched. dark star fixed beneath skin.)
Mercury: quick-silver god. slippery signifier. hot/cold. sick/well.

Well. S
     i

        c

            k.

Cadmium: yellow paint.
Arsenic: springs we soaked in
        winter nights, *Ojo Caliente*.

We didn't know about americium, cesium, perchlorate, or PCBs.
We didn't know about hexavalent chromium.
We didn't know about selenium (its soluble & insoluble states) or selenosis.

I, too, was once "highly mobile in water."

                        Consider, now, the lyric possibilities of being
          "re-suspended
               in high winds."

It Is Documented

Someone saw ..patches of.. . hair... ..grow back.. . ..discolored… …
Someone felt. .the forest .shuddering.. Someone .. .realized... .soils..
and. ..grasses were. .. particularly...radioactive… …Someone .. heard
.. .undeniable. ..rays of… .light… Someone .knew.. the thinking ..
had not yet focused.. on.. … .long-term. ...effects …Someone felt ..
a tear.. in the. ..meaningful .. . folds and… ..persistent.. . fatigue…
Someone saw the .. . will to .. . self-reflect in .. . real .. … time was ..
. absent…Someone… knew .. surveillance was .. . limited to .. …. .
observation .. .external appearances .. .and veiled. ..non-specific .. …
questioning   ..Someone heard a voice .. ..entangled. in … . hair..
…Someone.. knew .. . an operator's view.. . within a ..hot... . cell ..
was ..accomplished through .. .. windows, …a series of .. ..mirrors,
and … ..retractable.. periscopes… … Someone realized ..local factors
and the … central.. .nervous .. .system.. .intersect .. … . ("a few..
people were.. … overexposed ..but.. they couldn't.. .prove it … and
we couldn't. . ..prove it… .. – so.. . we just.. . assumed.. …we got ..
away .. . with it").. … Someone saw.. … fallout .. .snowed down on
… familiar.. surfaces… for days .. . after ..the … .. blast.. …. ….
Someone knew. .. local residents.. ..collected .. . rainwater … . off
their roofs .. … .. into .. .cisterns and … .. ..drank it.. … Someone
knew .. … …(it is documented) .. . . it rained .. .. the night .. ..
after ..the test … … .. .Someone knew .. .. the local people ate peas,
.. .root ..vegetables, … .and corn from their .. .. .gardens, … drank
the milk of goats. ..and/or .. …cows.. … … Someone knew shoes, ..
…clothing, ...floor coverings, ...vacuum. cleaners, .. . children's..
toys, ...and .. diapers were .. contaminated… …Someone believed ..
.. (o.. *someone* believed).. a normal .. . person.. could ….probably
stand.. two to .. …. three times .. . this amount .. …without
sustaining…. ..permanent ..bodily ..damage.. ...Someone swore .. .
fatalities .. . would not result… unless .. ten or more .. times.. . this
dose .. . were.. .delivered.. …Someone knew .. to wear .. ..

respirators,.. .to evacuate .. ..themselves. ... when high exposure..
.rates.. were.. ... measured,.. ..to close their… .windows and .. .
breathe… through a .. .slice..of … .bread.. Someone recognized the
.. .. Creator.. .(Brahma), .. the Preserver. ..(Vishnu), the .Destroyer..
(Shiva)… Someone muttered "those poor.. . little… .people, ...those
poor… .little people" … … ..Someone. vomited .. in the shrubbery,
.. while others .. .danced and.. .. flashed . the .. . victory . .. .sign …
…Someone chose the .. . Jornada .. . del Muerto.. . east of the.. Río
Grande .. .for the test ..site... .. .Someone reported being .. a passive
and .. . detached. ..spectator at.. ..his/her own death. .. .Someone
cried out .. .. … "Batter   my   heart, three-person'd God!" …
Someone saw the mind … a .matrix for light, ...a lambency of .. …
Someone realized .. . the past, ….retaining the fever of .. . a ghost, ..
lives.. .. in the present .. ..Someone whispered … .. . "In the .quiet of
.. the night, .. . in loneliness, … .in stray.. moments,.. at .. .stop
lights, ... on elevators, .. . we may finally give .. . into .. .and admit
to .. . our..mistakes, ... our .. . ... inadequacies." … Someone. ..
understood ."it is the soul … .. in the dignity of .. .its.. . humility,.. ..
which we find .. .. beautiful".. …Someone said .. .. "I ask you for .. .a
light… ..You give me … .a light"… .Someone ..realized.. … cells
deteriorate.. .. .at different rates.. so .. .. .the moment of death is.. …
..imaginary.. …Someone ..believed . .. .in a flower's.. . inner..
unassailability … Someone consumed … more oxygen during dream ..
..than .. . awake.. … .Someone asked "If the study showed .. thyroid..
… .cancer .. .four times higher .. than.. .. .elsewhere, …would a full-
scale.. . study . .. .be. .. .conducted?" .. … ..Someone responded.. .
"Cancer rates ..are .. . one piece of .. information… ..considered"

Someone felt.. .a flutter in .. the.. .temple's .. .veil

Elegy to a Baby Albatross at Midway Atoll

(ocean gyre: plastic)

(to be navigated with a magnifying glass)

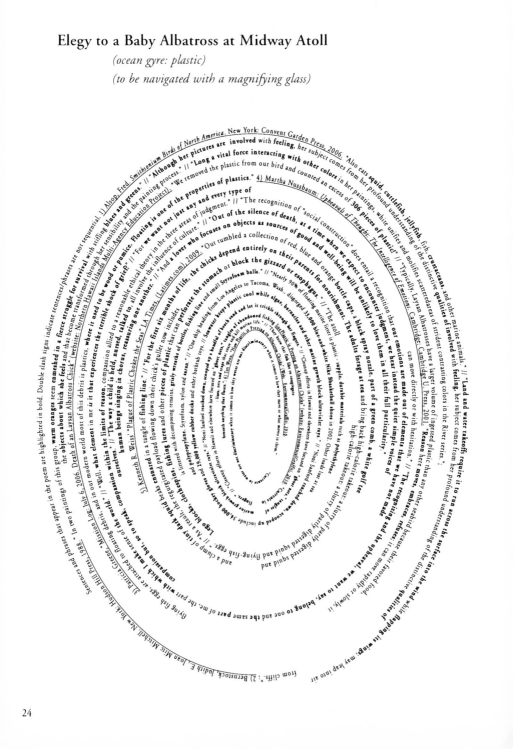

For the Record

re: *Los Alamos Historical Document Retrieval Assessment Project,*
Public Meeting, June 2009

[Public: Is there a model that your group is using
to calculate . . . threats of multiple exposures over
a long period of time?

> LAHDRA Review Panel: Detailed estimation
> of public exposures . . . is beyond what we've
> been able to do . . .]

[Public: Who is doing risk assessment for the
LANL releases . . . ?

> LAHDRA Review Panel: Right now, nobody
> is.]

[Public: If we move forward with a dose reconstruction . . . how much
expertise does the peer review panel have with regard to addressing small
rural populations? . . . And we are concerned about gender equality
on the peer review panel. We think we need some women, some people
of color. We need some diversity to reflect northern New Mexico.

> LAHDRA Review Panel: The problem is, quite
> frankly, in terms of experience in health physics,
> radiation specialists, there are not many
> minorities or women in the world.]

/// //

"*Soy* _____ _____. *Soy de Mercedes del Norte. También, tengo*
sangre del Pueblo de Taos. Tengo unas preguntas y traigo un consejo.
Pongan esa información en las lenguas de la gente de aquí. No
solamente en español, pero en Tewa, también and in the languages
of any other Pueblos that surround the Jemez Mountains.

My point is,   *(I'm not sure who is listening)*
yes, I am bilingual,
    but this information isn't . . .   *(It doesn't matter what language)*
You are missing the point:
    to get this to the people   *(if one doesn't want to listen)*
who need it the most . . .
Even before (the first building)
            even before   *(If you don't understand)*
the experimentation,
            there was   *(it's one thing)*
impact on the local
community. They were forced,   *(If you don't want to hear)*
some of them at gunpoint,
            to leave   *(that's another)*
their homesteads. You don't
even mention . . . on the maps,
        obliterated   *(I'm not sure who is listening)*
from history. The trauma
            (inflicted)
continues,   *(It doesn't matter what language)*
and is measurable,,,
is an issue (liability), and needs   *(if one doesn't want to listen)*
    to be studied equally to
exposure to
plutonium, tritium, or anything . . .   *(If you don't understand)*
The division continues. .. .
                                            (that's one thing)

we still have people
        on the Hill,   *(It's another)*
and people
        in the Valley   *(if you don't want to hear)"*

/// //

["Hello, my name is ___ __ _____ _____. I'm
a nurse in the Española Valley. I'm very concerned about
the health effects of Los Alamos, but what really struck
me was that plume of the Trinity site. I had talked to my
family about this before because 25 members of my family
have died of cancer as of today. When I saw the plume,
the plume floated to exactly where my relatives are dying.
That is, the Salinas Tiwa and Piro Pueblos, that land was
stolen from us, actually—the Abo Land Grant and the
Alamillo Land Grant. Not only was our land grant stolen,
but our health was stolen, also. I had never seen the plume
as you showed it up there, so I'm thankful that you showed
me that. I'm looking at the report and it just struck me very
hard. It really hurts my heart, also. Thank you!"]

___ __ _____ _____ is thankful   *(and we lower our heads)*

to know why 25 members of her family have died of cancer.

Thankful

(and we bow down)

to be shown on a screen filled with light

the path the plume floated

and hovered,

27

hovered

and floated

over tribal lands

(and we eat the earth)

II.

Most Mornings

                      I woke slightly out of breath. Winded from the ghosted
run between the land of living and the country of my death, I'd drag my dreams
behind me, from bed to desk, write poems of sleep and ink and newsprint.

Ah sleep. Sleep and summer smoke.

From its cage, the fan purred a noisy exhale.
The mocking bird outside our bedroom window
      sang in all the local tongues and dialects.
Your car, leaving up the graveled drive,
      made for a lonely sound—
                  and a relief.

The dog would rest his head on cagey front paws,
      make an effort at patience. The appliances would be truly patient
         though full of curiosity
            about what might come next.
The doorbell might have rung
               if we'd had one.

We'd listened to the forecast. Sony by the bed and bath.
Bose above the compact discs and art books.
Radio news unleashed and born again.
Thank god, we'd say, for the "on" and "off" switch.

Then one night a voice from dream announced,
In one or two weeks there'll be a catastrophe.

Winds were driven.   Waters rose.   Levees broke.

What will you take with you? the dream
        asked. *Myself,*
               I said.

Sunlight Hardens on the Bed

In the next room,
handmade cabinets open, shut. A crashing sound
and the man's voice calls out *glass*. Scalene, obtuse,
with a generous curve. Another woman's voice
from the speaker-phone enters. They are stringed instruments,
so events happen quickly. The spatula scrapes against
the body of the skillet. The brain rewires itself
tonographically, as though just being someplace warmer
could change the music. Fire at will, he says,
when they return to the house on the mesa
in a sky like ice water, stars tinkling. Shards
reminiscent of sails, and he carries the broken
in a box alongside the kitchen island and out
the back door, its window tracked by drippings
summer oil left. Nothing to protect either of them
from the heart's investment. Divested of all else,
what she learns will be survival
without guilt. What he learns will be startled
dependence on   the not   mapped .

Worlds inside the World / (position in suspension) / Tearing

Alma   in   the   hospital   .

Perhaps
                will   come   home.
Perhaps
           not.

Got   up.   Ate   a peach.   Checked   my breasts.   Nothing   un-

usual.   They are
                            my   friends;   they are

                                            aging. Tree

rings   with   trails

                            the worms   left.   The breasts

still   hopeful,
                round   in   fruit   & buoyant,   becoming

wine-filled   sheep's   bladder
                                            swung

                            down
when   I   bend.

Standing up.   Lying down.   Feeling   'round

mis tetas   with   three

                                     finger   pads—

Gentle beans , ,, soft peas . .. .

The dip

(beneath)   each   nipple   a sudden

                                                drop

                                                  ,   mysterious

water.   Swift or

                    easy   current.   Darkness of   no
more

       floor.

               Of not
     touching

                 bottom.

                        Here — — or

there   — —

              in the river.   Feet   with
ankles

       & heels

               & arches   & toes

like fish &

      my long legs   from which   they   suspend

in murky   brown   or green,

                              depending

on time of   day or   night,   & the   light   angle.

Stone   on the   far   side

                              — — another   woman — — not
Alma,

but   like me
                    a friend to   Alma — — sits.   The wooden   cross

            carved ;
                         how it   blends,   its weathered   grey

amid   watercolors,
                         sprouts of

electric   green.   Not tall   as I   am

or the   cottonwood is.   She

                         doesn't like   thorns.   I'm   not

wild   about   this   current.   Though I dreamt its

surge

            before

our   journey   to

```````the   river.      Swam with

focus        toward   the   dock   ( inside the dream )

``````````````````` that seams

a rock  along   the waking    shore.   I am

a cross-hatch

        in    motion,    entering

riffles

        shallow    stones   made

                    that    in   my   d ream    was

                                    river   thickening

into a dangerous-

                    to-humans    weave.    Horizontal *and*

vertical

            scrim    skimming fast. *Alma !*  I shout    & cross

the first    current

                    like the first     sleep      before

        the light

switch      came.   Hesitant

&  in the end

                unwilling     to try     the second, not

yet .  Giving in—no,

                *letting go*     bit by     bit   Alma     her   grip

on position

                in suspension. Falling

                                off

into    carried away,

                        one with  the tongue.


I don't know

but trust   in
                    something
                            ancient.   How like

2   slight   reeds
                    Alma's friend

       & I

          gather at the river.

2 strips of  shell  white

         mixed with  madder  root,  yellow ochre

& sienna.

Alma in the hospital  w/ seven  tumors in her

       breasts,  an obstruction and a  mass.

Is Alma  dying of

cancer  ;   is Alma

       going to be

      well ?

## How Strange to Wake

after long illness.

Your dog of eighteen years
out back in a grave
next to a tree
not yet planted.


Under a blue moon
the drive north
through Blood of Christ mountains,

hauling the *other* body—your own body—in the back of a red Subaru.


How strange to wake after all that . . .


A small door in the brain opens into color.

Surrounded by darkness—inside—
*that's* where we lived
all our lives
in that tiny Techicolor room

inside the inside of the dreamer's head.

# After Having Thought About It for a Long Time

In the warm springs where they
bathe and float together
her hand accidentally touches
his hand underwater.
His head jerks up in uncertainty,

while her face remains nonchalant.
She draws back in a flutter
of sand, though on second thought
what she wants
is to take his hand

in hers, open
his palm to her mouth,
kiss the upturned flesh,
press palms together—
map to inner map, interlocutors

to separate pasts
locked in deaf-mute
languages of distress, frightened
by the sudden explicit gesture,
yet sprung open, exposed,

and imprinted with desire
to touch the beautiful strange forms
that grow from their upturned bodies,
innocent and supple as algae sprung from
alchemy of water, light, stone.

# The Light Would Have to Draw Back

into cloud
the dust gather itself      into mesa
for us to still hear          its far away      traffic
followed by rumble        the blast not getting ahead of itself
though loud      quite      and the blowing apart

its scornful rejection      occurs   in complete    silence
broken through by the furnace
ten miles hotter      layered        so   well
now clearly      the object        the un-signaling
of that critical assembly          the glow
its ionized air          less red the swirling

dust disperses from its stem
its question mark of a        column
and the steady gaze of animals    and minerals
the singular verse of      at us    and the smoke clot
shape of the North American continent   famously
the *amanita muscaria*   deflates    small    sunless

bright now      though almost colorless      (the men return
to the wombs of gentle  female
dogs    the mother-mattresses cradle
the gadget        deconstruct its wire
and drum    un-beat-upon)
light grows      alters      shapelessly

the shimmer in the desert            the edge of   sand hills
so it looked      so it seems again
the danger modest   given the weather
the sun      even while shining
slides back    into predawn   July 16, 1945   without
sound      and then

# Three Quick Piercings to the Heart

You were holding me (in the dark).
I wanted to cry out "_____, my heart
hurts."

                my eyes were closed

        I was swimming
                weightlessly (sometimes recklessly)
                        around (in the dark)

My night searched day for explanation.
Did I walk too far?
Did I move too fast?

In the morning, my heart flops, fish-like, beached.
Where fish drown on the atmosphere, my heart suffocates

(for *lack* of air).    You are gone
and I am where you were.
Wrinkles in the bed,
concentric miniature waves,
a vast open shore of leaves.

The pillow like a heart, slightly twisted
'round itself, a comma or a whale.

# Inland See (II)

re: *"Deepwater Horizon" catastrophic oil spill, June 2010*


Grandmothers scoop up a light-net,
haul pelican (in the spirit world) like fish—
and fish. Or net the sludge,
thick ooze, and how-to
staunch a puncture. (Sometimes
we must protect ourselves, we said of television,
internet.) Our fingers
over dinner, splay—were we? Eating a bird,
we become it.

# Life Stories, & Other Possible Endings

*Spring Valley, Nevada*
*(in the shape of a bristlecone pine tree)*


The way at night
as we eat  and drink … next to a river
cool currents of air.. slide  between us…as though someone has rolled
down the window in a fast moving cloud…  .. across the desert .. where you are town
guide  of   abandoned mine sites… . and trees alive from before Christ—their seedlings
sprung  about the time democracy    started up in Greece… Everyone (except women
& slaves) gathered in the amphitheater .. to cast votes .. a field of single hands raised…
We are surprised  ..  to see small daubs . . . of forest brushed by quick painterly
strokes.. .. ..Or like animals  .. you say .. a herd of zebra or gazelle clustered… The lion..
no longer hungry . . . dozes sleepily at the edge of the lake.. … while  power lines rise
in pairs their arms crossed one over the other .. range to range .. in a procession resembling
Kachinas … (the gods  have assumed modern—though still electrifying—expression)…
. . . You press the final elements into . . . the tail of the car . . . while like a  puzzle
I wander—a bit  of  a river rain—about the edges of ground … where we've filled
our heads with stars—*such a relief!*—next  to the stream ..where we've laved cold water
on our  freshly naked  skin .. each morning after sleep….
        Beneath the smooth and oddly human   curves of a pine  struck  by longing
and apparently.. .once upon a time, by lightning  ..        we say the little    *thank you*
prayer to    montane        life … .

                            to  twisted bristlecone
                            and purple monkshood ..
                        to yellow stream
                        violet and the
                        hardly startled
                            doe  we stumbled
                        on. .. .that first
                        morning …
                            golden-mantled
                        .. morning . .. the way
                        we used to do   when we
                        were a child – the last,
                            the very last thing

## Water. Light. Stone.

1.

The ponderosa past the glass was planted for him, and yet
it was a gift for me. What river took us or what current
in the grey of dream? Lift me silk and feel along—
between—amid the morning pool of lines. I sing of *this*.
Recall when I could walk into the gorge—its maw—climb out.
(Was it my fault I lay me down with such determination?!)
The slightest speed, too many steps, and I'd be ill as hell
again. Inside this terrarium of restraint, I am a romping letter,
an alphabet of hope within a cold disastrous soup.
Chill and bitter broth, you ask? Green, I say, and lemon.
Pliant trunk of radish. Onion peeling veils. The kale
(of course), the kale. A simmering of olive blood. Its fiery
amber. Though twilight's blue, this time is round and orange. The ink
is black, its chamber long and silver, and similar to sleet.

2.

My surface now like snow gone slack. Patches, paws, boot
& claw tracks line the road. A muddy rust—not bright enough
for blood—pocks & stains the slush. The road itself, pure ice,
pure sheen beneath the slap of silver chains on spinning tires.
Our puppy wildly casts about. His curly hair, his grey-black
pads, slip & skate. His easy four-foot gait contrasts
my regimented limp—not a limp at all—but slow
and measured glide, a metric meant to match my thumping heart,
its pulse amid the sage. Needles on the snow-shagged
pine commence—fall into—gusts. The whim of Chinook wind;
a forest scarf, its silver fringe of willowed boughs. The stiff
salute of apple trees, their shuddering sap-drained limbs.

3.

The warning signs that burden dreams of snow
and driving fast, too fast along the seam of mountain road, the icy
bend I skidded from adrift and calm as flakes, their blanched
and frozen blood crystallized as window panes that fall and fall
and don't care where or if they pause. Below, is a hidden place,
where bodies branch and rivers dark and sleek will smoother stones,
or ruffle them with lace around an absent pulse. Don't linger there,
where leaves begin to mulch. Get up and *move*, but slowly now,
in undertones of bud and grass that patch a wounded earth.
Greening it, whatever it may really feel (what does it feel?) beneath.

## Bernalillo County Creatures

because they are wild    they startle
the river right outside the door    sultry    muddy
like an earless lizard    my wedding ring
its wet self and the hermit thrush I once was    flushed outward
willows in shallows we waded
you and I a molecule    from somewhere    a tear

the river doubles back
inside itself
plastic nudged into wild grass    otter sands
and then    our chatter

## Natural Enemies

*i.*
When ceiling fans swim
                    in an    aviary    circle
                                without ceasing,
            they    create
a liquid
        suggestion  , with
                        a steady    black      center. More solid    than
                                                    the dog
                                lying on    tiles
                made of clay,      enamored of        sunsets
and
impressed                by the memory   of
                                    goat    hooves ,
            pads
                    resembling      rose    petals,
                                a dog's        underfoot.


A    dog    is    no      different than
                            a human      when sleeping.
Its torso    breathes,    deeply
                            it heaves,      and    dreams    its foot
            into
                        movement,    swift
and sudden
                & so  distinct    from
                            the   uninterrupted
            nature  of
                                a fan's                    radiance.
The dog's    foot    touches

                              a  wooden            leg
                                        carved        to the shape
of a  lion's
            paw                  &  lies
beneath
                  the chair
                                        as though  for
                                        protection
                        from heat,
                                        not  from
wings   of
            the fan          hovering
above. A cat
                  will   have        nothing
                                              to do
                                              with it. A cat has
lived
                  and      died          in the   shadow  of
wings
                  and will      never       be        comfortable
with    a ceiling
                        fan, no matter

the temperature.


*ii.*
Water     depends  on      temperature
to cut
            a fever.
                        A fever depends on    trees

                        to        keep a    river   cool. Never
mind      the        shade, we
                              will
                         swim  in        the glitter
that insists
on
                    a temperature.
Our temper
              finds    itself   shaded
                                        indoors,
        where  fins  spin
                         a cooling      story
      of  a  summer    lagoon. The dog
                              done with      his
                              dream
is   inhabited   now    by
Nirvana.
Deep
         sleep—
                              For a while, to be
without   quest         is      relief.
A dog
         wakes,
                    re-lives
                                   everything
to grasp
              its bearing.  Bears
              and dogs   are
related
by
                    their snouts. When

          we     dream
                of
                          another,      we want
to       be in           touch.
                    One    state                touches
another
              because
              underneath
                              the states
                                      is
              a continuous
                        continent
and  to die
              is
              to be
                          content in this.


*iii.*
As to live is
              to push
              up/against          a shelf. The mountain
is
          young   &   still
                          growing        higher. When
one
              shelf     slides ,,,,      beneath, fans
          of fir &
                    rocky      shores
                                    erupt.  Ringing
          in the ears

                                        might be          one
            bird          calling
                    to another. Two
fans,
            one in     each          room, stir       up
wind
                    with their fins.
                            We wake          like
a dog
            from      dreams          we        don't
remember— —
                    Inside        the story        of
                                    a fin  in        relation
                        to                    a        mountain,
an eclipse
                    may   occur. Inside
                                    a temperature    of
  illness is
water
            at the end   of   a    road,    mirage of
undulations,
                    wind shears,


                    a mother,
natural enemies,
                    not


                    the soul    alone.

# After Listening to Fanny Howe Online

Her words connect me to my rooted self. Beaten
in childhood.     Descended from    the Beats
and their   run-over-you-with-a-truck   sexism.
A lover of     beets, their dark     blood
and     sweetness. Newly    oxygenated  and veining
the leaves.    Oh     thank you ,    poet ,    for  saying
it  straight, with no interest    in      fooling     anyone.
I'm a    romantic   because    if      truth is    beauty
I can   bear  it.    I *like*   smoke  and   mirrors.
Throughout   the   Southwest
the air   is    dry and    smoke-filled   at   night, thick
in  our    nostrils, not     a bad   smell    and   why   would
it  be, coming    from the    enflamed   forest, not
chemically   laced from     the  Lab. Not
a    claustrophobia-inducing     early-summer-
of-the-century   fire   when we had to    drive   an hour
north to    breath  freely. Is    this     what    freedom is?
Freedom to rip     a    hole in      the   ozone,
shred the   sky-gauze ?   No     god
up   there;  god is    here  crying,
or    nowhere   at   all.   I     prefer   to think  of  *her*,
a  sudden    apparition of   stars  in  a   bed
of mysterious    and   compelling  darkness,
able to   disappear and    reappear as
called-upon, to    float   from   one  locale to    another.
A thousand-foot    crack   in     the mesa
or  a    constellation. Frankly    reassuring,
so    you sense    the poem    is    ongoing
even   when the   ink    ends. I    don't have   a    romantic
attitude   about endings, I    am    too close
and can't   imagine that    anything   I'm going   to

do   will   change   that,  though   small   things
matter. Even     Linda,    who      lives on
next to    nothing,    manages   to      dress    well.
She has    pride   and steps up    to    the plate
in the face of     beauty. Its   moon      reflection
and     promise. That's what     beauty    does,
it promises     something   you want to     follow.
I could not live    in   a   city   or   a   bus    and argue
with the   Bible.   The Bible  is     too much
shadow. It    weighs    me    down
with the    magnitude of    its   matter. All   of the
light  got    distilled   out of   it    and released
into   the   ozone. Its    Kali   matter   and
alchemical   lead. The burden     of    its
cadences. People    wandering    here and    there,
nomadic. The sun     never    shines in    the Bible
because  it  was  written  in    the desert.
Jesus had    kindness   in   him    and  was  a   trickster.
S/he  had to   be mercurial    as    the moon
to   survive.

# When the Poisons Begin Doing Damage

*You Pause*
in the doorway, look back, observe.
Inside the stucco is a house, inside the house
is where you live—a dwelling smeared with lime,
the air dusted with cement product, and so
your swollen throat, inflamed lungs.


*You Flee*
Stain your composure:

        rattle away in your blue Subaru aplomb, a less

and less tight assemblage, the dirt road

        another form of imminence. To the west,

the gorge: its beckon and shale.


*To the East:*
town. Its buildings composed
of %$@!+ and metals stolen from the ground.
Everywhere disorienting reflectors.
A crew of convex mirrors. Red, blue, brown.

Synthetic is the glue that holds
the straight up. Pastes it upright. Bond beams
and floodlights. Walmart and Walgreens.
Only the Pueblo and Church of St. Francis de Assisi
seem made of their natural impermanence.

Forest. Straw. Clay. Sand .. .

A bucket of water
from the spring.


*Revulsion, Sets In*
You are (a little) afraid of your whirlwind,
its counterclockwise movement from the past,
so you head responsibly east, to the town, to the job. ..
You intend ,
but at the edge of—
At West Romero Road & Hwy 68, you can't

(I mean it isn't what—
*okay*—
it repels.)


        *The Unconscious Issues a Warning*
        [      the dream snaps you awake.
        Says: get up now, pack toothpaste, your black cloth bag
        with local market insignia, books,
        lucky underwear, and favorite all-purpose cup.

        Says: refuse a brain-full of lesions,
        a liver full of lead. Panicked? No—
        focused, with an edge.]


*In Order to See—*

no, not see—

In order to *enter*
        her, you
whirl—make a u-
turn,      set off
across
the open mesa
to the eight-hundred-foot-deep
gorge


*You Press*
with your toes in their
shoes at the edge of the snake-slit
tear    into the immediate
cracks    dark entering    places
between rocks
absorb through
each iris
the undulation
shimmer    of stone
composition    cliff sides    in
movement
winding
in sea-like    waves
below    and    all    around    until

*Now*
you can give it   full   rein
this that you feel
for her
in her wilderness   form
her ancient and nearly   waterless
ocean   floor, overcast ,
benightedly  undercast


*You can*


breathe


her air, its  cataphatic   movement


against skin,   your hands


*What a relief to open   her garment*
*to enter her   raiment: its sophia  and sage*

*Blue hills rise to mountains*
*The roll and curve, if earth*
*be her*
*in the round*

# III.

# From Here to There: Imagining into the Ruins

*Myrtos, Crete*


she dawdled her way up mountain     a slight mountain
less slight    if you began    as    a    fish    circling
in the sea    below    she circles    the      carefully

assembled    &    stacked    limestone      red schist    dry mud
& sticks mortared   together      stones   contain     presence
watchful   it was very hot     water spilled from the
cistern    1700 BC    a giant

unseen     mouth   bit   into   the curve    of its    cell    for
the next   350     years of    contained
occupation    no    one    repaired   it   did the
Minoans   think   the goddess did it    on purpose

a great     breast spilling     its milk    our seeker    sings her
way back to    her    air-conditioned    room    to assuage
a   frightening    exhaustion   she listens to    a
poet -*    via    internet   & dips into    sleep

at    the    phrase    *under-mothered world*    thinking    *that's it—*
*that's    why   I   came   here—i was hoping*     *to find*

         a mercurial    soup-spoon    engorged with    condensed

milk     rises    from the turbulent    sea    of her

             dreaming
                 mind

*/// //*

up   a limestone   step-street   down a   spilled-grass breeze-way   blades
and  thorny   weeds   scratch her   calves  her shins  she makes  a turn
into  a bite-sized   room and   thinks  very possibly
she   could live here   wonders if   they  would let   her   have  a
window   she would like  a  window   onto   the courtyard
and  moreover  the sea  its blue   every-day   would calm
the chunky   orange   stone of  reverberative fears  she
reflects   on the cellar  its gypsum  walls   resemble
Styrofoam   blackened from   the burn  water  soluble
slabs   waffled  scrunched   and call  to  mind  wooden  columns  of
the palace   flared   hair
                1450   BC   flames
                        ....   a
small
          cistern   at the base of  a winding   staircase   a
spiral of   bone  in  the  rib  of   Pyrgos Hill   she makes
her  way  in search of  purple  light-wells   their  marbled  limestone
discs   punctuate   corners   of a   bronze  age  mother's  home

*/// //*

waves feel   their  way  up   the  shoreline  at night   a
woman   in the next-door  apartment  sings
opera  in the mother  tongue   the guide-
book   says  there  were   only a  few
Minoans left   by   300 BC   but
our  dawdler-poet   sees them   everywhere
on this   remnant  island   their  silhou-

ettes   their   snake   goddess   features   in
the shape of   a   young   man's   head
his ears   long   tubular
neck   as   he   welds   orange   flags on
popsicle   sticks      at a      construc-
tion   site   along   the      National Road
to   Agios Nicholase         or in   the
curve of   nose   frescoed   build of   women ac-
cepting   euros   for   water   potatoes   eggs
onions   and   figs   in the   Monday   Myrtos   marketplace


*/// //*


in   the   Ierapetra   museum   a      statue of   Persephone
from   2AD      holds   an   ear of   corn   in her   left   hand
her   head   crowned by   a   small   altar      encircled
by snakes

*When   I   call   them   they   come*
she says
                to no one   in   particular.


*/// //*


sometimes   language   comes   to   her      she sings
the Minoan   site of   Pyrgos Myrtos      when   only
wind   brushes   the   ancient   settlement of   serpentine

our   poet   traveled   all this   way to

touch the ruins     of a    house     fire

*dear mother   would you please   write    to*
*me   in as much   detail    as    possible*
*tell me   of   your    childhood   & the*
*shake-up   that   so     marked you    left   you*
*vulnerable    to    Achilles   &   that    brutal   gang*
*of   so-called   Superheros*

                              the   Minoans   are    silent
or    perhaps   they    are     only    shy and
she is     listless    impatient
even among     ruins    what    grows   is
photogenic    choreographed    a flowering
in hollows of     thorny   burret    fennel   &
asphodel    lutea      wild sprouts
and seeds

              if    she could    find
a     *sibilant*   angle    to    the      sea beyond
the   villa   along   the   jumble of   steps
across   the    tapestry   of — a    royal    runner
scrolls    alabaster      and
so   often      she   is   tired
all    over     Crete   cicadas
hide   in    trees   a   chorus of    aggravation

*/// //*

in   the   middle   of   the   night   when   it   is   cooler
she'll   recall   the   bees      at   Mycenae      buzzing   a-
round   a   leak in   the   mouth   of   a   bright   green   water
hose   and   the bees      will make her      think   of   the   bee   pen-
dent   and the bee   pendent will   recall   the   tholos
tombs   and   the   tholos   tombs   will   call   to   mind   the   om-
phalos .. .. ..

## We Are Standing in Her Field of Vision

She has said what we want to say. We will name our unborn after her.
She has said it, said it already. How can we say? How can—
We have to in our own river, brown its body, green its shine.
Long ago its lava, it is still falling, it is still tipping, it is over-edged,
it is moss face, it is algae grown, it is lichen in us, it is licked place.
In our own blood flooded, how our heart thuds erratic to it.
And she was there, and he was there, for a long time we worshipped
out the west window, worshipped where the river ran its icy fingers,
its rumpled whirl, its white curl and larval world. For a long time
we dreamt it in us, dreamt it through us. It was always there singing

# The Self as Conduit, Not Locale

The dead lived here once.
Under trees and silver roofs
glaring up at the sun, fish-shaped leaves burn.
Branches, slender and delicate, thicken with paint.

If this town was a woman's body. .. ..
If this avenue was her spine .. . .

                              At night, smoke floats
up the road, past a blue door, the black sash of window sill
to the sea.

She is deranged, hypothermic from rain
and wandering the streets with a candle, a cup of hot tea, milk.

The great stones have lines in their faces. They lie down
next to the water to wait. An old woman
in a pink bathing suit looks away—

# Little Shifts, Here and There, a Fashion of Change

Now, the sound of a bulldozer
                              in the desert air,
A throb preceding reversal.

Now, the yellow shriek, a white semi
                              hauling a load of adobe
Up the midmorning breach
                              of the hill.

The eye, like a wasp
        is caught
             in its mud-walled cell
                              of requirements.

My feet are cold at night
                    and grow flimsy at the foot of the bed,
                                        caliche and soil,
The diligent back beat of weeds
                         among arrhythmic flowers,
While the grass remains stiff
                         in spite of this two-bit rain—


*/// //*


If I had this day, I'd draw blue strokes across it
                              with a watercolor brush
And live between each of the lines
                    —"dramatic
                         and wholly convincing"—

with a sliver near the end for translation
And a wide stretch in the middle
                    to lie on the unmade bed
        and read or listen to the rat-ta-tat storm
                as it moves
                    from window to window.

But I am a drunk
                wandering between two lanes
                            of slow moving traffic

In a small town in the late fall just after dark.

Blotches of water
                    slide down the pane
With such stopping and starting
                            such jerky irregular music
The skin of the piano
                beads—


                        /// //


It's difficult to live in a town full of tourists, in the suffocating eye
Of a storm,
                at the center of a vigil in the desert,
                                        close to the ceiling, in this heat
Where the "hourly wage"
                    and a "living wage"
            do not correspond—
                        like letters

Between two young words
        brave, but already broken—

Or a bridge from which
        the *other* was thrown.

Or where flight, by way of something remarkably human,
Is tired        discarded and        attempted in snatches—

On a good day, I listen to a recording belonging to no one
        and dream
                of the previous color of my hair.

I'm an hour late, the traffic has died,
                and a few birds, here and there, are rejoicing.

It's also Tuesday. My mother is alone
        with her new yellow dog,
                        while I work
                in a lime-colored room off the plaza,
Homesick, and tapping the keyboard with two fingers,
                in a manner not at all unlike
This *matapolvo,*
                this day-after-day
Merely killing-the-dust rain.

## And Afterward, to Eat Oranges

—to dust off the dark spots of oil
and clean my face.

A draft, sinewy and luminous
         wraps across our vision.
In a haven of smoke, cars throttled past.
*¡Qué silencio en las iglesias!*  Someone
on a phonograph plays the cymbals, tapping them lightly
as in a dream when you kiss me awake.

The clamoring of spirits springs up inside the piano.
What are we waiting for, those of us who hear?
Already a waif with torn clothes and a finger,
I want you like a tight fit, like a swallow under eaves.

# Understand Me, *Sir*, Romanticism Undergirded Each Act

We were younger, we laughed
at the girdles, giggled in the face of
the fit and what it meant to embody
the feminine— —how to cleave act-
tually meant to press
to a part,

and fall into
the HOly MOther of

desire ( just thinking of it
made her wand exist ! ) .

When you ask, in sickness as in health, the readiness
of my *yes* becomes
a woman at sea
in the sage
and at ease with it. Fronds in the peri-
pheral  cheer on the matter.

# The Phallic Hand of Gaia

Last night the wind scrawled around as I lay down. You were already sleeping
  the deep sleep of a wild clam, your hand flung across your chest,

a creature the tide spumed up, the rest of you plunged in the footfall of dream,
  practicing for death—

On this day of our earth, your hair has begun to fade. Such an ocean of light
  in the room, strands of you are shaded. Your olive skin and *gitano* eyes.

Our lustrous sheets and tiny *huerto* in the sage, a languor of green.
  The flowerbed leafing out—bush by bush—like the women you scent

your life with. Mornings, early and often we make sparks, make fish; before
  sleep, during the night, and always on waking, the wave of you curving

into the crevice of me. Gentle, you rise in the sea-dawn of mesa, beyond the
  lattice of window-screens, the silk they make of the world before sunrise.

Easy to imagine the sea, the swerve of its shore. You abandoning our bed
  to lay out your nets, their patterns of ardor on sand; patiently

and with such pleasure, you sit naked and amphibious to tend them. It's all
  the same to you, you are so sensual and delighted with existence.

Whereas I am often in my head, like a lighthouse displaced in the desert. You
  have to coax me into arboreal splendor, the matrices of fuchsia and lime

you tend in our courtyard; the wild crinkled roses and yellow cinquefoil next to
  glass doors and cracked sills; the commotion of dogwood in the corner,

its arterial-red stems in winter; and the penstemon plant, its lubricious purple
  trumpets, *tilted*. Funny, how the honey-locust refused its own

effulgence, until the past and I made friends, and maybe—possibly—
  everything was forgiven.

# That Briefly Containable Love between the Sun and the Earth

It wasn't your Moorish arch that first attracted me, though I came to recognize it
as part of your signature, no different than exposed peaks and islands, or the roomy
pools of your eyes, by which the animal inside could be enchanted and removed.
There was a fine crack to the finish of our meetings, a rhythmic clack that swelled
the wood and sealed the seams—marked by lightness or brilliance of expression,
though you would always be the cynosure, and I, the oneiric and revenant one.
Seamstress, counter-clocking a way back from the mask, I lay there screen-side,
horizontal as a transept, and yet with the usual unpredictable manners of fortune,
able to throw off the curse. Ours was the courage of mossy growth in the desert,
by which tossed off stones in the nearby gorge became enlivened. We were river
koans, finished to match the leaves. Like 丞 coins, we windowed the center.
Unwilling to move, we let worlds stream through. It was warm-up and cool-
down in the go-for-broke sensation of debts piling up at the start of a century
of fire. Followed by water, and the softly plagued shape of our irises in spring.
It's true, the rosette of your seed-head by nature occasionally wandered, while
escape of your fish in pursuit of the showiest flowering plants remained a quest
cohesive with my own. My heliotropism and your pantheistic animism are hands
in the shape of a prayer. As long as you are dipper to my bowl, I will be a waterfall
rising, in a universe made of number, made of song, on loan.

## Everything Begins in Sacrifice

You keep thinking the dark-eyed junco will move,
lift or swerve—but its limbs are groggy from rain
or having recently woken as you did from omens
flying up in your face, as though from a poem
thoughtless of time and everyone sleeping,
silent and seeming content
to be still, except, of course, for the water
that rolls from the roof in the absence of gutters—

*/// //*

And cuckoos that turn into woodpeckers.
Such sensitive and intelligent eyes.
On the other side of the glass
among leaves, their wings
pull close to their warm yet silver-grey bodies
braced against rain and the sense
of a probable blow;
while masking tape peels
like a bandage no longer needed
from the wall,
                    this house,
                              this unfinished room,
this dark in which you are alone
with the queen and the lady-in-waiting,
deeply embedded, yet plainly revealed
in the sheets. Those magnets
on the door in the kitchen,
they are also living a double life

of buttons controlling the music.
Too loud, in fact, overwhelming as the night
settles in, a presence
with one red light amid every other.
You recognize the signals.
We all know exactly what's out there
and approaching from inside of us.

You think: at least it's not throbbing,
at least it's just *on*. What a forlorn wait,
this business of being an eavesdropper
in a night-time conversation
that everywhere else is a mid-afternoon
of amplified voices—busily knockin' em out
—though *not here*, not here on the speaker-phone
to which no one is listening;
and the voice that fails to arrive is your own.

*/// //*

So you're rumbling along, half-awake and half in a hurry
as though the old truck with its rusting sides
just might have motivations, trajectory,
momentum through the fields
surrounding our lives. Beneath wet leaves
and cotton-less cottonwoods,
the low flying bird doesn't look up,
doesn't rise quickly enough
and your reflexes have grown slow

for such a young thing, while you slept on and on
in the dark. The faint sound of something
flattened. Followed by the awkward,
half-fallen from its hinge. A rear-view mirror
of wings. Marred now. That's it.
Glued by their own sticky juice to the
too bright sheen, this strip of road
over which a merciless, half-awake human being—
that is, these days, yourself—has gone.


*/// //*


And you'd like to fall in love
all over again,  minus half of the pain.
Forget it! You remember that city, Zaragosa?
Sitting back on the big couch
in the hotel lobby and thinking of her,
and why she, who is so "beautiful," and "compelling," and "talented"
is perpetually—what shall we call it?—*alone.*
Behind you, he talks to his cousin
on a phone reaching up to the room
where the actress recovers
from each night's performance,
while you know, you *know*
Love always involves a wound. So we stay
in a cheaper hotel on the plaza
where the walls are three-quarters window
with green billowing curtains
full of mid-winter sun,

because you love to make love
while other people are walking
below, at a clipped pace, on the white marble tile—
the sound of their shoes and their voices,
a half-foreign language, everything
you do not know. The fact is, you savor being an island
in the midst of a thunderous river—
the Ebro, isn't that right?—
rushing past on all sides.

# Back There, at the Back of the Room, a Missing Friend Is Repeated

I think I fell in love this time in front of a t.v. I never could follow

In a glass drained of all but the sound  thinking *Well, I'll just eat  a little more of that*

While the middle of the day presses against the inside of my blouse

Half-way to our knees among mirrors your ankle bracelet minus half of my flesh

We are both of us lonely on the other side of this conversation

My dire indiscretions and irony the metallic sun of your happiness dress

How lonely is the gym of the mind on the body's weekday schedule

And the circular strain of our see-saw holding hands

The naked ice shakes in your hand me with my little wound you

With your make-believe wedding such composure and daring at once

## A Sand Trail w/ Stone Walls & Configurations

For a while I am walking along a path
next to a river. A sand trail
w/ stone walls & configurations.
I dream more prosaically at night
and for a while I am aware she is following.
Then she is no longer a poet, but a lion.

The house is bright and quiet when I wake,
and I hear water draining from the bath.
Some days I am a morning bedside chatterbox.
Others I am on my way south to see the
great whales. That's the circumstance
in which she is at her best and most natural.

In a house made of wood, the main task
is making collages—she has a box-full,
though I think to myself, *no thanks,*
*this life is not the circus for me.*

At one point I go for a walk near the ocean.
At the stone dock a speed boat races past
and crashes into what is called a jetty.
I think surely there will be injuries and admit

there are moments I envy the alcoholics,
the way they do that disappearing act
into something else. A man shoots
a very old very loud gun in every
direction. It is a way of keeping time,
the equivalent of church bells.

She was so handsome I felt completely,
almost completely unworthy. And when she went
into the sand dunes and I heard a cry,
I was afraid. I raced to find her, but no
need to be distraught. She was content,
leaning against a large stone beside the river,
complicated, in the shade.

## I Have Known Her Since My Beginnings In Her Thoughts

as slender-fingered with an octave reach. An *aster-*
*risk* in her uterus. I am tall and narrow like the god,
except for my snake-goddess breasts. Hard
to believe I ever fit inside my other
woman of many fits, which had little
or nothing to do with belonging,
belonged instead to feeling trapped.
My mother winds along a path in the forest.
The stiff snake of her walking stick punctuates this ground.
Trail of her ellipsis: new moons, coin-shadows, periods,
chocolate mints.

# These Last Left Notes at the Start of Departure

We keep busy moving our fingers, joint by joint, an exploration,
w/out moving past our peter-pan collars, our green eyes trained
on the everlasting ravine. We're afraid, we've forgotten
to ever glance skyward, to look up like a telephone book
with a blank face and no numbers for dialing, or a bank
from which all money has flown. In some desperate
and unfeeling corner our stars are suspended; a relative
dawn takes years to arrive. It's enough to keep reaching
into the coil of the burner, a poisonous snake
bent on chasing itself. Listen, on the other side of
this curtain is power, pulling our hair—yours and mine, both—
up by the roots. I tell you the speaking trees are a frenzy;
hair beneath our arms is a nest growing softer with age.
My hip hurts from a future of too much rain and your neck
has grown longer, but let's not talk about illness—not now,
not ever—it's a terminal chamber in a room full of mirrors:
the other side of clouds and underside of rain. Our light
approximates the wattage of candles; we have a right
to go walking like anybody else, along the too-warm
path of our previous hurry-up making (such a cost, such
a nerve-wrecking cost). I'll admit, I had some idea
of leaving, by way of lifting like those overrated balloons
on a Sunday afternoon—ah, but here comes the sun again
anyway, with its glaring but affable stare, burning lines
like a still unwritten letter, in the desert of too much
and always the same old. This morning the shapes of
our faces are returning. For the sake of a silvery minnow,
a willow, or even a thorn, let's keep on—including
low flights and too many houses—while the annunciation
pours into our bodies. Here, in this once wild neighborhood,
the animals, two by two, begin to reappear.

# En Su Tinta

One or two letters from my mother and the taste
Of my lover's skin I can mother my mother now
Because of his fingers dreaming this in a shower that is not
The color of sea and yet reminiscent of stamen stacked
Orange in a mistral explosion of flora I can never remember
Their names or a tree full of figs the pigment of which
He is painting the changeable face of the sea a cloth
Cast over the table spread with apples and peaches
The buoyancy and merry up and down hieroglyphics of
Cheer his brush that is verdant opulent porous
Missives from she who is mother of encouragement and seed
The feisty coast a faraway emanation of voices
Luminance of mothers and daughters and sea

# IV.

*. . . the book itself, the volatile scattering. Spirit.*
*—Stéphane Mallarmé*

*I cure with language.*
*—María Sabina*

# Fallen Moon in the House of Speech / To the Shade When It Is Missing

*In autobiography, I matter. In the post-autobiographical world, I am matter.*
*—P. Hampl*

1.
A solitary raven, black against blue,
                    rim to rim,
          early that morning she dreamt of
                    herself being beaten—well, not beaten,
          but slapped around—a little—as a prelude
                                        to
                                                  sex.

          The bride descending, etc.
                    stripped down,
                              broken, the urge to be taken
                    apart—again—to be separated, that's all
                              into something
                    a little less solid, yes.
Spread like a fan or run of cards—
                    the deck of a ship
          loaded
                    and bearing down:

          *Oh moon, small small moon*
          *Adrift, a tilt on my watery floor*
          *An unseen light shoots down on you*
          *Looking up like a face, a flat pearl.*

          *There's a gun in my mouth*
          *And you are the target—*

She can hear them—the disenfranchised, the locals—
          someone's uncle, and father, and cousin—above, on the rim
               of the Río Grande gorge she's heading down into—
                    her eyes on the edges—compulsive,
Perhaps, neurotic—the repeated glance up—on the watch,
               the slow or fast hand,
                    for who or whatever
          amid smattering of juniper and pine, stubby bush, cracked
               lines, a silhouette or shadow,
                    the stunt man peering over,
                         (as though this were a "Western")—
In a nearby ravine
               they're shooting appliances.
               —*whine* and *retort*—*whine* and *retort*—
Ahead of the game, they *practice*.
The dead Frigidaire and rusting Westinghouse
          are brought to their knees
               among bottles, broken
          in the hard glint
               of sublimated revenge,
While the eight-hundred-foot drop
          from mesa to river
               is blurred by dust,
          and a subtle shudder
               in the late-in-the-a.m. yellow.


2.
The mind requiring a hand,
               yet gentle with damage—
     the tip of a finger, a dart full of ink

or something
on its way in a hurry.
(Her sunglasses rest on the desktop at home,
while her keys are splayed—
perhaps tired
of a ringed existence—as the clock,
whose heart stopped
sometime in the eighties,
is digitally red.)

*What of that?*

The hair on her arms stands
a wheat-field from the flatlands.
The roar from behind—a bullet-shaped
shadow with wings—dropped so swiftly
into the crevice—in its glide, a sound
violent with absence of living, no pausing or parsing
not even a turn or a tip of its brim—metallic
and stiff with indifferent skill, the un-feathered wing—
not just a plane—but a B52.

*Does it help*—as they say—*to give it a name?*
Though, *just practicing, just practicing*
maneuvers for the sake of the "They" and the "Us"
that keep being altered
amid colorful television titles
for each post
millennium   war.

*Who ARE those guys?*

3.
Between walls of the gorge,
          rocks might begin moving.
Above.    Below.    A detour—
               here
and

               there—
          around boulders
                         already
               fallen,
          some time        thank god
               when no one was around.


At night or late afternoon,
          everyone—well—even the homeless are working
                    sides of the street, while out here in silence
          (except for the wrens, the migrating blues & midmorning reds) giants
               have thrown
          these stones down—ENORMOUS—the size of *VWs*—
               in annoyance or play
                              or  RELIEF.
Meanwhile, the river and roar of its white hair
          and leaves spilling over
                    stones at the lowermost reach,
          not-so-still waters, not-so-green-
                    or-so-silent murmuring
                                   the shoreline.


Do the dead grow gray hair deep in their caverns?
          Or, is that a metaphor (can we really say *just?*)
                    for consciousness—spreading out—a little
          decomposition, or thawing, a coming
                    apart

4.
It's the stones that are cracking,
         the bride amid all those dark lines
                  descending again the staircase,
         her fractures blurry with motion,

her hard-bound copy of Janson's
         *19th and 20th Century Art*, an ancient edition.
 Spine a little off, a little broken at angles,
         hair falling out
                  like straw from the red cloth cover.
         Inside those pages, a solitary—or nearly so—
                  *femme* (Louise Bourgeois),
         once  lived on chocolate
                  on the Lower West Side,
         where phallic shapes rise
                  like sponge from the porous
         stone of a museum enclosure,
                  cells of old farmhouses
         full of the instruments of ailing,
                  (as though this *were* an old "Western")
         even though
                  the maker was French and terrified
         of
                  TOO MUCH SPACE.


5.
Continues, our walker.
         The road busting up
                  in terms of vehicular traffic,
         reclaiming its natural
                  rutted from run-off curving
         between cliff sides closer and closer to water,

not the end, or at least

never *not* the beginning,

blue where the light has not yet arrived

or has already disappeared.


6.

Why that?—why her mother

calling—

frantically—it was

to her, in her sleep?

Though on waking—what?—it was really—*oh damn,*

herself

raising her voice

at her sister,

again, long distance, on the phone

—hopeless!—the flimsy door

black metal latch

doesn't catch, doesn't catch

but keeps on slamming (in the wind).


7.

The phone rings.

One is tempted—

on a day such as this—not to speak.

Even in the face of beauty.

Whose face is that? The mask

becomes frail, collapsing in on itself
at the corners. Cold rushes inward
              to town, while dark heads disperse
on a wind-scattering plaza.
She hides in the house—an old woman in a car—recalling
              the bumper-sticker: *Keep Your Laws Off My Body*,
                          the first woman she ever loved *that way*,
              the red Fiat forever breaking down.


8.
She'd like to write of the way back up,
              round of the corner,  and lover
                          whose figure is instantly
              identifiable, strolling eagerly into the gorge
                          to meet. An *Orpheus and Eurydice* moment.
              She *is* returning—maybe not all the way—at least
                          she'll never be the same—


9.
Recalling the bed
              she kept falling into—attempting to rise—
                          while the unseen
                                      dropped roses
                          over the rim. Roses kept hitting—
                                      *landing*—no,
*Hitting* her face,

As snow

       from an early spring sky—light

          falling onto her

                  eyelids—could not stay open

       —tried and tried—could not—


Following, now, the river—

              her fate—

       as in *obligation*

      willfully chosen—to enter—

Or shall we say

             *it entered her* as the music

Turns into singing

             under the impulse

     to make notes.

# Notes

"*Da-ma-te*, Demeter": the word/phrase "*Da-ma-te* " is in Linear B and is the earliest known spelling of "Demeter."

"Inside a Dream, Inside a Storm to Come": was inspired by W.A. Bentley and W.J. Humphreys' *Snow Crystals*, (Dover Publications, 1931).

"Cochiti Lake, 1989": see *Plans and Practices for Groundwater Protection at the Los Alamos National Laboratory (LANL), Final Report*, (The National Academies Press, 2007).

"It is Documented": derives from the *Draft Final Report of the Center for Disease Control's Los Alamos Historical Document Retrieval Assessment (LAHDRA) Project*, (June 2009), with the exception of the lines beginning "In the quiet of the night" and "it is the soul" from *Masochism: A Jungian View*, by Lyn Cowan (Spring Publications, 1997); the question, "If the study showed…" and the answer given, "Cancer rates…," which are from commentary at a public meeting held in Pojaque, New Mexico on June 25, 2009, regarding the LAHDRA project; and, the lines "I ask you for a light. You give me a light," from Paul Valéry's "Poetry and Abstract Thought," (translator, Denise Folliet). The phrase "a tear in the meaningful folds…" is a reworking of Mallarmé's "meaningful folds and even a little tearing" and the final line, "We felt a flutter in the temple's veil," is also a borrowing from Mallarmé, who used the phrase in his essay, "A Crisis in Poetry," (translator, Bradford Cook). The essays by Valéry and Mallarmé can be found in poet and editor Melissa Kwasny's marvelous *Toward the Open Field, Poets on the Art of Poetry, 1800- 1950* (Wesleyan University Press, 2004).

"The Light Would Have to Draw Back": is a reversal of physicist Otto Frisch's description of the Trinity explosion, found on pages 10-19 of the *Draft Final Report of the Center for Disease Control's Los Alamos Historical Document Retrieval & Assessment (LAHDRA) Project.*

"For the Record": is from commentary heard at a public meeting held in Pojaque, New Mexico on June 25, 2009 regarding the LAHDRA project. The two persons quoted at length have endorsed this shaping of their testimony.

"Most Mornings": is in mimetic conversation with Muriel Rukeyser's "Poem." See *Rukeyser Out of Silence, Selected Poems*, (TriQuarterly Books, 1992).

"How Strange to Wake": is in mimetic conversation with Charles Wright's "Three Poems for the New Year." See *The World of the Ten Thousand Things, Poems 1980—1990*, (The Noonday Press, 1990).

"Natural Enemies": the lines "When we dream/of another, we want to be in touch" owe inspiration to Michael Burkard's poem, "Before the Dark." See *The Entire Dilemma*, (Sarabande Books, 1998).

"From Here to There: Imagining into the Ruins": the phrase "under-mothered world" is ‑* Brenda Hillman's, from her poem, "Air in the Epic" in *Pieces of Air in the Epic*, (Wesleyan University Press, 2005).

"The Self as Conduit, Not Locale": I owe a debt to Leslie Ullman for this title.

"That Briefly Containable Love between the Sun and the Earth":
I am grateful to *simple fountains: for indoors & outdoors, 20 step-by-step projects*, by Dorcas Adkins. " 巫 " is the character for a
shaman (wu), and first appeared in oracle bone inscriptions of the
1600 BCE Shang Dynasty, China. *Wu* were associated with white
magic and were believed to possess healing powers often expressed
in incantations. During the Zhou Dynasty (starting around 1100
BC), the term *wu* referred specifically to a female shaman. See
*Dreaming in the World's Religions*, by Kelly Bulkeley, (NYU Press,
2008), *Witchcraft and the Rise of the First Confucian Empire*, by
Liang Cai, (SUNY Press, 2014), and *Chinese Shadow Theatre:
History, Popular Religion, and Women Warriors*, by Fan Pen Chen,
(McGill-Queens University Press, 2007).

"Fallen Moon in the House of Speech / To the Shade When It is
Missing": the epigraph is from Patricia Hampl's essay, "The Smile
of Accomplishment: Sylvia Plath's Ambition," (Iowa Review, Vol.
25, Number One, 1995, p.11).

Photo: Brian Shields

Sawnie Morris has been the recipient of a Poetry Society of America George Bogin Memorial Award and, for her chapbook in *The Sound a Raven Makes* (Tres Chicas Books, 2006), a co-winner of the New Mexico Book Award. Her writing about poetry and poets has won a Texas PEN Literary Award and has appeared in *Kenyon Review*, *Contemporary Literary Criticism*, and the *Boston Review*. She is a co-founder of *Amigos Bravos: Because Water Matters*, a non-profit advocacy organization for the waters of New Mexico, and she is a frequent contributor and past Book Review & Essay Editor for *Taos Journal of International Poetry & Art*. Sawnie lives in northern New Mexico with her husband, the artist and environmental activist, Brian Shields. *Her, Infinite* was a finalist for fifteen national contests prior to selection for the New Issues Poetry Award.

# The New Issues Poetry Prize

Abdul Ali, *Trouble Sleeping*
2014 Judge: Fanny Howe

Kerrin McCadden, *Landscape with Plywood Silhouettes*
2013 Judge: David St. John

Marni Ludgwig, *Pinwheel*
2012 Judge: Jean Valentine

Andrew Allport, *the body | of space | in the shape of the human*
2011 Judge: David Wojahn

Jeff Hoffman, *Journal of American Foreign Policy*
2010 Judge: Linda Gregerson

Judy Halebsky, *Sky=Empty*
2009 Judge: Marvin Bell

Justin Marks, *A Million in Prizes*
2008 Judge: Carl Phillips

Sandra Beasley, *Theories of Falling*
2007 Judge: Marie Howe

Jason Bredle, *Standing in Line for the Beast*
2006 Judge: Barbara Hamby

Katie Peterson, *This One Tree*
2005 Judge: William Olsen

Kevin Boyle, *A Home for Wayward Girls*
2004 Judge: Rodney Jones

Matthew Thorburn, *Subject to Change*
2003 Judge: Brenda Hillman

Paul Guest, *The Resurrection of the Body and the Ruin of the World*
2002 Judge: Campbell McGrath

Sarah Mangold, *Household Mechanics*
2001 Judge: C.D. Wright

Elizabeth Powell, *The Republic of Self*
2000 Judge: C.K. Williams

Joy Manesiotis, *They Sing to Her Bones*
1999 Judge: Marianne Boruch

Malena Mörling, *Ocean Avenue*
1998 Judge: Philip Levine

Marsha de la O, *Black Hope*
1997 Judge: Chase Twichell